D is for Dinosaur

A Prehistoric Alphabet

Written by Todd Chapman and Lita Judge

Illustrated by Lita Judge

Sleeping Bear Press wishes to thank and acknowledge the following people
for reading and reviewing the manuscript:

- Michael J. Ryan, Ph.D., Curator of Vertebrate Paleontology at the Cleveland
  Museum of Natural History and Chief Paleontologist, Phaeton Group

- Jerry D. Harris, Ph.D., Director of Paleontology, Science Department, Dixie
  State College, St. George, UT

Lita Judge especially wishes to thank Dr. Ryan for his assistance and review
of the final manuscript and illustrations.

Sleeping Bear Press®
310 North Main Street, Suite 300
Chelsea, MI 48118
www.sleepingbearpress.com

© 2007 Sleeping Bear Press is an imprint of The Gale Group, Inc.

Printed and bound in the United States.

First Edition

10 9 8 7 6 5 4 3 2 1

Library of Congress Cataloging-in-Publication Data

Chapman, Todd.
D is for dinosaur : a prehistoric alphabet / written by Todd Chapman
and Lita Judge; illustrated by Lita Judge.
p. cm.
Summary: "Our prehistoric world is presented from A to Z and includes
information and current theories paired with illustrations of each topic. A poem
introduces each topic and is accompanied by detailed text for further reading"—
Provided by publisher.
ISBN 978-1-58536-242-4
1. Dinosaurs—Juvenile literature. 2. Alphabet books. I. Judge, Lita. II. Title.
QE861.5.C53 2008
567.9—dc22   2007025445

In 1811, when the study of prehistoric animals was just beginning, a 12-year-old girl named Mary Anning uncovered one of the most important fossil discoveries of her time. Mary's brother had found part of a skull exposed in the sea cliffs near their home in Lyme Regis, England. Mary searched later near the skull and uncovered the complete skeleton of what looked like a giant sea monster. She led the excavation despite dangerous rock slides along steep cliffs. The creature was over 165 million years old. It was the first ichthyosaur (ICK-thee-o-SORE) known to the scientific community.

Mary's father had died when she was very young, leaving her family to a life of hardship and poverty. Out of nine children, only she and her brother survived. They lived during a time when most fossil collectors were gentlemanly scholars, but Mary and her brother started selling fossils to help their mother pay for rent and food. Mary went on to discover other new species of prehistoric animals, including the first plesiosaur and the first pterosaur in Britain. During her lifetime, many called her "the greatest fossil hunter the world has ever known."

A is for Anning

Mary Anning found fossils
in the cliffs by the sea.
When she was twelve years old,
she made her first great discovery.

A
a

Mary Anning searched for individual fossils, but in some places thousands of fossils are found tightly packed together. This is called a bonebed. Bonebeds give us clues about how dinosaurs lived. Some bonebeds give clues that a herd of dinosaurs drowned in floodwaters of a violent storm. Their bodies were deposited on a sandbar. Then meat-eating dinosaurs and crocodiles feasted on their carcasses, leaving tooth marks scratched into bone.

The river sand and mud then buried the carcasses. Over millions of years, the sand and mud turned into solid rock. As water seeped through sediments and into the bones, minerals were deposited, slowly replacing the bone with rock, turning them into fossils. So a fossil is a rock that used to be bone! Dinosaur teeth, eggshells, even feces (called coprolites), and footprints can be fossilized. A fossil is a trace of any living animal or plant. They give us clues about different kinds of plants and creatures that existed. By studying them we can learn how big dinosaurs were, if they ate meat or plants, and if they walked on two legs or four.

Bb

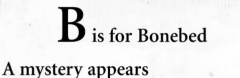

B is for Bonebed

A mystery appears
after millions of years.
Thousands of fossils are found
buried together in the ground.

Uncovering fossils can be a long process, requiring careful work. Paleontologists first prospect over fossil-rich land, searching for new sites. Once a location is found, a team of people may need to use jackhammers, pickaxes, and shovels to dig through huge amounts of rock. Then fine chisels and brushes are used for excavation.

Fossils can be delicate once exposed. Special glue is used to seal them, fill cracks, and strengthen them before final excavation.

Fossils are often taken back to the lab still encased in the rock in which they were found. Larger fossils are wrapped in plaster-covered burlap strips for protection. Sometimes the block of fossil and rock is so heavy only a helicopter can lift it out. At the lab, technicians use magnifying glasses, small drills, and dental picks to free the fossils from rock. Then the pieces are delicately cleaned, studied, and assembled.

C is for Claws

Slashing, slicing, cutting claws—
giant claws, longest claws!
What strange creature had such claws?
The thought of that should give us pause!

The longest dinosaur claws ever discovered were two and a half feet long! They belonged to *Therizinosaurus* (THER-a-zeen-o-SORE-us). But very little is known about this dinosaur. Paleontologists aren't even sure what this dinosaur ate or how it used its claws. Perhaps they were for protection or ripping open termite mounds.

Most dinosaurs with long sharp claws were carnivores (meat-eaters). They ranged from the smallest known dinosaur, *Microraptor* (MY-cro-RAP-tor), two and a half feet long and weighing about as much as a crow, to the largest meat-eating predators that ever walked the land.

Some of the deadliest hunters were members of the dromaeosorid family. They weren't the largest carnivores, but they had speed, intelligence, and saw-edged teeth. Their greatest weapon was an upturned sickle-shaped claw on the third toe of each foot, perhaps for slashing open the bellies of their victims. They might have hunted in packs, working together to kill larger prey. *Velociraptor* (vell-OSS-ee-RAP-tor) and *Deinonychus* (die-NON-ih-kus) belonged to this family of dinosaurs. But perhaps the deadliest of them all was *Utahraptor* (YOO-tah-RAP-tor). Its razor-sharp toe claw was at least 12 inches long.

The word "dinosaur" was first coined by Richard Owen in 1842, an anatomist who had been studying fossils of prehistoric animals. He compared the teeth and bones of *Megalosaurus* (mega-low-SORE-us), *Iguanodon* (ig-WAHN-o-don), and *Hylaeosaurus* (hi-LEE-o-SORE-us) and noticed they had characteristics in common with modern reptiles. He decided they were not lizards, but belonged to a group of prehistoric land reptiles. The name dinosaur comes from the Greek words *deinos* meaning "terrible" and *sauros* meaning "lizard."

The Mesozoic (MEZ-o-ZOE-ik) era was known as the "Age of Dinosaurs." It lasted from 245 to 65 million years ago and was divided into three major time periods: the Triassic (try-ASS-ik) from 245 million to about 205 million years ago, the Jurassic (jer-RASS-ik) from 205 million to 144 million years ago, and the Cretaceous (krih-TAY-shus) from 144 million to 65 million years ago.

During the Mesozoic, thousands of different dinosaur species existed, but not all at the same time.

D is for Dinosaurs

There were fearsome meat-eating tyrants
and plant-eating, earthshaking giants.
Tiny raptors and giant titanosaurs,
so many different kinds of dinosaurs.

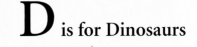

Dinosaurs have been divided into two groups based on the skeletal structure of their hip bones. Saurischian (sore-IS-key-an), or "lizard hipped" dinosaurs included both carnivores and herbivores (plant-eaters). They had a hip structure with the pubis bone pointing forward and the ischium bone pointing backward. Ornithischians (or-ni-THIS-key-an), or "bird hipped" dinosaurs were all herbivores. They had hip bones with the pubis and ischium bones both pointing backward.

Dinosaurs hatched out of eggs. Fossilized dinosaur eggs range in size from a one-inch-round golf ball to about 18 inches and elongated like a loaf of French bread. Eggs can't grow much larger than 18 inches because the shell would become too thick to allow oxygen to pass through and the embryo inside would suffocate. This means some dinosaurs, like a baby *Argentinosaurus* (AR-jen-TEEN-o-SORE-us), were the smallest babies relative to their mother's size that walked the land. Even if it hatched out of the largest egg possible, it was tiny compared to a mother weighing up to 100 tons.

Dinosaur names that appear capitalized and italicized, such as *Saltasaurus*, refer to a specific genus of dinosaur. These names often end in "us." Names that are not capitalized or italicized like sauropod, titanosaur, and dromaeosorid, refer to a larger group of dinosaurs. For example, *Saltasaurus* is a dinosaur genus that belonged to the larger group of titanosaurs. And all titanosaurs were a kind of sauropod.

E is for Evolution

Escape!
Impossible to do.
For mammals just evolving,
Troodon eyes are watching you.

About 230 million years ago dinosaurs started evolving from archosaur reptiles. Evolution is the process by which animals (or plants) gradually develop new and varied features. For example, some dinosaurs evolved longer necks for reaching higher food, others evolved longer claws for better hunting. These features were passed on to future generations, until eventually new species evolved from earlier species.

This doesn't happen over a few years. It can take thousands of generations for a new species to evolve.

During the Mesozoic era, mammals were small, trying to get a foothold in the world. Most were the size of a rat. The largest was only as big as a border collie. Over time, mammals adapted and evolved to dominate the world, but during the time of dinosaurs, they were "the hunted." Dinosaurs like *Troodon* (TRUE-o-don) preyed on them for a bite-sized meal. *Troodon* was highly advanced with large eyes, perhaps for hunting at night. They were possibly the smartest dinosaurs with the largest brain size to body weight.

When dinosaurs were first discovered, scientists never imagined that modern birds could be closely related to these prehistoric beasts. In 1860 a German scientist discovered *Archaeopteryx* (ark-ee-OP-ter-icks). It was the size of a blue jay and had feathers. Scientists didn't consider it a dinosaur and put it into its own category as the oldest known bird.

Also in the 1860s, Thomas Henry Huxley began noting the similarities some dinosaur bones had to modern bird bones. Scientists debated the connection of birds to dinosaurs for over a hundred years.

Then, in the 1970s, John Ostrom compared the small *Archaeopteryx* skeleton to that of *Deinonychus* (die-NON-uh-kus), a 10-foot-long meat-eating dinosaur. He was amazed by how similar the two skeletons were despite the difference in size. Some scientists grew bold, predicting that we would someday find dinosaurs with feathers.

F is for Feathers

Dinosaurs with feathers?
Imagining this is not hard,
now we know they still live
as birds in our backyard.

F f

Their predictions came true in China in the late 1990s when *Sinosauropteryx* (SINE-o-sore-OP-ter-iks) was discovered. Then *Caudipteryx* (kor-DIP-terricks), *Sinornithosaurus* (sine-or-NITH-o-sore-us), and *Beipiaosaurus* (bay-pyow-SORE-us). These were all dinosaurs with feathery coats!

These recent discoveries have convinced most paleontologists that dinosaurs did not go extinct; some are still alive today as modern birds! This has dramatically changed how paleontologists think dinosaurs behaved and what they looked like.

Feathers are rarely fossilized because they are so delicate and must be quickly covered in fine grained sediments to be preserved. Most dinosaur fossils are found in sediments too coarse to contain fossilized feathers. But the fine sediments of China have preserved enough feathered dinosaurs to show us that they were common in a group of dinosaurs called theropods.

Many scientists are starting to believe other closely related theropods including *Velociraptor* (vell-OSS-ee-RAP-tor), *Troodon* (TRUE-o-don), and *Oviraptor* (oh-vee-RAP-tor) may have also had feathers. Perhaps even *Tyrannosaurus rex* (tie-RAN-o-SORE-us rex) babies hatched with downy coats!

G is for Gigantic

Growling, gruesome
Gig-a-not-o-saur-us!
The biggest meat-eater
ever known to us.

G g

Imagine the meat-eating *Giganotosaurus* (jig-a-NOT-o-sore-us), with its eight-inch-long teeth, bending down to look through your second-story bedroom window! Bigger than *Tyrannosaurus rex* (tie-RAN-o-SORE-us rex), it was the largest carnivore to ever walk the earth. It was up to 50 feet long and weighed as much as 16 pickup trucks, eight tons!

The larger carnivores were probably not swift runners. Instead of speed, strength was their weapon. Perhaps *Giganotosaurus* hunted even the most giant-sized herbivores by biting their flanks with dagger-like teeth and waiting for their prey to bleed to death. They had a keen sense of smell and probably also scavenged for carcasses. They roamed the land like ferocious vultures, sniffing out their next meal.

Giganotosaurus lived about 100 million years ago in South America. Recent discoveries in Argentina are breaking all records for the largest, heaviest, and longest dinosaurs that ever lived.

H h

With predators like *Giganotosaurus* on the prowl, many herbivore (plant-eating) dinosaurs, traveled in herds for protection.

Herbivores were a very diverse group. The most common were hadrosaurs (HAD-roh-SORES), the family known as "duck-billed" dinosaurs. Their mouths had rows and rows of closely packed teeth (almost 1,000!)—perfect for eating plants. Other herbivores had fewer teeth. Perhaps they swallowed stones called gastroliths, just as birds do today, to help grind up and digest food inside their bellies.

Herbivores also included the sauropods (SORE-o-pods). This group of dinosaurs was the tallest, longest, and heaviest animals ever to walk the earth. They had tiny heads, blunt teeth, and very long tails and necks. Their huge bodies housed enormous guts to digest tough woody conifers. The largest sauropods might have eaten a ton of food each day. It was a process that produced a lot of dung and a lot of gas!

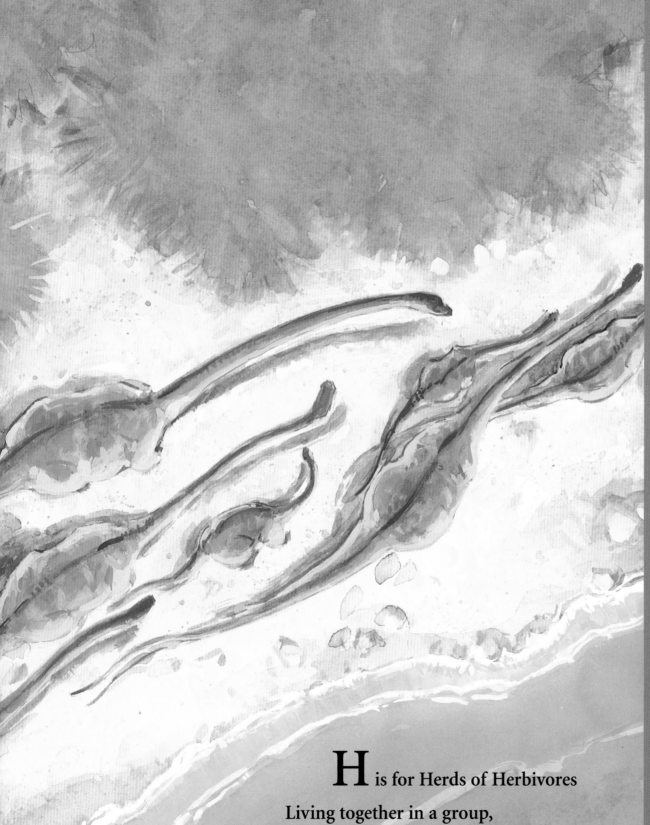

The longest sauropod yet discovered is *Seismosaurus* (SIZE-moe-SORE-us). Five school buses in a row would barely reach its 170-foot length. The ground must have quaked when it walked the land, giving it the name "Earthshaking Lizard."

Vegetation was important to dinosaur life. Plants formed the base of the overall food chain on land. Herbivores survived on plants, and the plant-eaters were food for the meat-eating dinosaurs.

Throughout the Triassic and Jurassic periods Earth's plant life included coniferous (evergreen) trees, ferns, ginkgos, club mosses, cycads, and horsetails. Many of these plants were very hardy and had underground root systems that kept them from dying even when the tops were eaten. This allowed them to grow back very quickly.

It wasn't until the Cretaceous period that the first flowering plants such as magnolias and palms evolved. The Cretaceous period also ushered in the first autumn color as deciduous trees (broad-leaved trees that shed their leaves during a season) like sycamores appeared.

H is for Herds of Herbivores

Living together in a group,
eating plants, producing poop.
Fearful of carnivores stalking in packs
waiting to launch their lethal attacks.

Many of the hadrosaurs, or "duck-billed" dinosaurs, had strangely shaped hollow crests on top of their heads, but the strangest of all was *Parasaurolophus* (par-a-sore-o-LOH-fus). It had a crest three feet long! Scientists made a replica of this crest and found they could make a sound similar to a trombone when air was blown through it. Could hadrosaurs have honked an alarm sounding like a brass band when a predator was near? Paleontologists think dinosaurs probably used vocal warning systems to alert the herd to potential attack.

The crests also seemed to have been larger in males. Perhaps males used sweet melodies to entice a mate, just like male birds. Could the Mesozoic swamps have been filled with the bellowing bugle of lovesick hadrosaurs?

Like animals today, dinosaurs probably used different sounds and calls to communicate with each other. Imagine what a whole herd of dinosaurs must have sounded like.

I i

I is for Intruder

Watch for danger, stay aware,
intruders lurk low out there.
When predators are seen at last,
sound the alarm—a warning blast!

J j

J is for Jurassic Giraffes

Dinosaurs evolved some mighty strange features;
that's why we find them such interesting creatures.
Some of the largest had heads really small,
but with fantastic long necks, they were five stories tall!

Some large sauropods were built like prehistoric giraffes with extremely long necks, perfect for grazing on the treetops! *Brachiosaurus* (brack-ee-o-SORE-us) was one of the tallest. Its head was 40 feet off the ground. Its size was its main form of defense since a grown adult was too large for most meat-eaters to kill. But its size had another advantage. Standing so high off the ground, it could browse for food out of reach to most dinosaurs.

Early paleontologists guessed that giant sauropods wouldn't have been able to support their weight on land and therefore spent most of their time submerged in water. They thought the nostrils on top of a *Brachiosaurus* skull acted like a snorkel. But scientists now think sauropods could support their weight and were land animals.

The largest sauropods were thought to live only during the Jurassic period, but recent discoveries have uncovered a few sauropods that lived in the Cretaceous, and they were even bigger! In 1994 four neck vertebrae of *Sauroposeiden* (SORE-o-po-SYE-don) were found. It may have been the tallest dinosaur ever!

K is for King

Tyrannosaurus rex means "Tyrant Lizard King."
It's not hard to imagine as a fearsome thing!
But would you believe a *T-rex* as mother,
or a family of four with baby and brother?

Tyrannosaurus rex (tie-RAN-o-sore-us rex), one of the largest, most ferocious meat-eaters, grew up to 46 feet long, 20 feet tall, and was as heavy as a six-ton dump truck! It had powerful back legs, but its fiercest weapon was six-inch serrated, dagger-like teeth. Its short, powerful neck supported a massive head with hinged jaws allowing it to open its mouth wide enough to grab smaller dinosaurs, shake them dead, then swallow them whole. *T-rex* may have also scavenged for dead carcasses using its keen sense of smell.

Recent discoveries are changing how we think of tyrannosaurs. The largest, most complete *T-rex* skeleton found was called "Sue" by paleontologists. Partial skeletons of another adult, a juvenile, and a tiny 200-pound baby were also found with Sue. Could this have been a family of tyrannosaurs? Paleontologist Phil Currie, from the University of Alberta, rediscovered a lost quarry site originally discovered by Barnum Brown. Currie found 18 adults, juveniles, and baby *Albertosaurus* (al-bert-o-SORE-us) buried together. Discoveries like these suggest that tyrannosaurs might have lived in large family groups.

The smallest known adult dinosaur was *Microraptor* (MY-krow-RAP-tor), only two and a half feet long. But the littlest dinosaurs were, of course, the babies. And the smallest ever discovered were baby *Mussaurus* (moo-SORE-us). Their name means "mouse lizard." No adults have been found of these dinosaurs, only hatchlings ranging in size from 9 to 16 inches long, with heads no bigger than a mouse! Paleontologists later guessed that the adults probably grew to over 10 feet. This shows us the drawbacks to naming a species using only a baby specimen.

Paleontologists once thought all female dinosaurs made simple nests of sand or mud, like many reptiles today, and left their eggs to hatch on their own. But new baby dinosaur discoveries have completely changed how we think.

Some dinosaurs hatched with legs that weren't completely developed. Like some baby birds, they were born weak and helpless. They weren't ready for walking. Imagine baby dinosaurs teetering and wobbling inside their nest, needing a parent's care.

Ll

L is for the Littlest Dinosaurs

These babies, just hatched from eggs,
have bones that are weak and small.
They are helpless and need care
from their mother, strong and tall.

Jack Horner and Bob Makela of Montana found the first evidence of caring mother dinosaurs when they found fossilized baby *Maiasaura* (MY-a-SORE-a) in their nests. They named the site Egg Mountain. The babies ranged in size from one-foot-long hatchlings to over three feet. Their mothers probably brought food and protected them against predators, earning a name that means "Good Mother Lizard."

Mother *Maiasaura* mounded sand and mud three feet high and wide enough for a grown man to lie inside. Each mother laid about two dozen eggs, but didn't incubate them—she was too heavy. Mother might have been caring, but she weighed as much as six pickup trucks! She covered her eggs with plants to keep them warm, like crocodiles do today. As the plants decayed, they produced heat like a compost heap, warm and smelly.

Maiasaura nested together, each nest just far enough apart to fit the mother's 26-foot-long body. It must have looked like a giant bird-nesting colony. Can you imagine the noise of thousands of babies squawking for food, and the stink of rotting plants and all that dung!

M is for "Good Mother Lizard"

She brings them food, she keeps them warm;
she guards her babies in their nest.
She stays alert as danger lurks—
This good mother gets little rest.

M m

Imagine a football field with so many dinosaur eggs you can hardly walk without stepping on one. This is what titanosaur (tie-TAN-o-sore) mothers left for us to discover over 70 million years later in Patagonia in South America.

Year after year, titanosaurs returned to an ancient riverbank to dig simple sand nests. Each female laid 15 to 40 eggs, tens of thousands of eggs all together. Titanosaurs were too large to stay and protect their nests so they left the eggs to hatch on their own.

Occasionally the river flooded, drowning the embryos inside the eggs. Some were later fossilized. Most years the eggs hatched and the sand slithered with thousands of babies smaller than their mothers' footprints.

By examining the embryos inside the fossilized eggs, paleontologists think they were *Saltasaurus* (SALT-a-SORE-us), an unusual kind of titanosaur with bony armored plates on their back.

N n

N is for Nests

Titanosaur mothers made simple nests,
    all clustered together in sand by the river.
When thousands of babies hatched all at once,
imagine how the sand must have slithered!

With several discoveries of dinosaur nests, paleontologists now understand how extraordinarily diverse dinosaur behavior was. Fossilized eggs, embryos, and babies are also teaching us more about dinosaur metabolism.

Early paleontologists thought dinosaurs were cold-blooded reptiles. A cold-blooded creature's body temperature changes with the outside conditions. Lizards need the sun to keep warm. As their surroundings cool, cold-blooded creatures become inactive and slow. They eat less than warm-blooded animals because they are less active. They don't sweat when they are hot and therefore need far less water.

Warm-blooded animals such as people, dogs, birds, and whales maintain a constant body temperature by burning energy created from the food they eat. As paleontologists study fossilized dinosaur bones, they are finding evidence that perhaps dinosaurs were warm-blooded. The structure of dinosaur bones reveals an internal structure more similar to warm-blooded animals like birds. Dinosaur eggs also show a structure closer to bird eggs than to reptile eggs.

At the beginning of the Mesozoic era, there was only one continent. It was called Pangaea (pan-JEE-uh). This giant landmass was surrounded by a single, worldwide ocean called Panthalassa (pan-THA-las-a). Over millions of years Pangaea broke apart and divided Panthalassa into separate bodies of water, eventually forming the continents and oceans we know today.

If we could go back in time and swim in the Mesozoic ocean, we might be surprised to see how similar it looked underwater to today's oceans. Jellyfish, corals, crabs and clams, sharks and fish were abundant. But look out! There were meat-eating marine reptiles. Dinosaurs ruled the land during the Mesozoic era, but marine reptiles ruled the seas. There were four major groups: ichthyosaurs (ICK-thee-o-SORES), pliosaurs (PLIE-o-sores), mososaurs (MOE-za-sores), and plesiosaurs (PLEESE-ee-o-sores).

Marine reptiles were true monsters of the ancient seas. Their ancestors lived on land, but returned to the sea to hunt for food. They evolved strong flippers and became great swimmers. But they were still reptiles, breathing air and probably coming up on the beach to lay eggs like sea turtles do today.

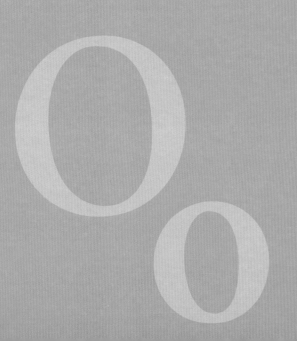

O is for Oceans

Monsters lived in ancient seas.
Swift and strong, they swam with ease.
They caught their prey unaware
but these strange creatures breathed the air.

P is for Paleontologist

Without the fossils in the ground,
would dinosaurs have ever been found?
These science detectives sift through clues,
always looking for something new.

Paleontologists are scientists who devote their careers to the study of prehistoric life. By uncovering fossilized remains of animals and plants, they closely examine ancient life and Earth's history. Their research has given us many answers about the fascinating world of dinosaurs.

Amateur fossil hunters have also made many incredible dinosaur discoveries but it takes years attending a university and studying subjects like physics, chemistry, biology, and geology to become a paleontologist. Studying continues when paleontologists leave the classroom and search for fossils outside where fossil deposits are found.

In the late 1800s two American paleontologists, Edward Drinker Cope and Othniel Charles Marsh, competed with each other, trying to name the most species of dinosaurs. They discovered about 140 new species, but their rivalry erupted into what was known as the "Bone Wars." They even resorted to blasting leftover fossil sites with dynamite to keep the other from finding new dinosaurs. Today paleontologists still aim to make new discoveries, but scientists around the world work together to uncover the truth.

Q is for Quadruped

Search for food on four strong legs.
Remain alert, look around.
Defend yourself against attack.
Kick and stomp and beat the ground.

Animals that walk on four legs are called quadrupeds. Quadrupedal dinosaurs were herbivores, varying in shape and size. Some were short, heavily plated, and low to the ground, while others were slow, massive, ground-shaking creatures. The largest known was *Argentinosaurus* (AR-jen-TEEN-o-SORE-us), a giant sauropod weighing as much as 17 elephants, 100 tons! Some herbivores spent most of their lives walking and browsing for food on four legs, but could rise on two legs to reach higher food or defend themselves.

Paleontologists once thought smaller quadrupeds, like *Protoceratops* (PRO-toe-SER-a-tops), were slow. They were three feet high and weighed about 400 pounds, but they were agile enough to defend themselves against swift hunters. A fossil discovery of a *Protoceratops* locked in combat with a *Velociraptor* (vell-OSS-ee-RAP-tor) shows the quadruped's parrot-like beak gripping its enemy's forearm. *Velociraptor*, in turn, has its back toe claw ready to rip open *Protoceratops*'s neck. Neither creature could escape. They were probably overcome by a slumping sand dune and buried instantly. Fossils like this are changing how we think of the herbivores.

The fastest dinosaurs were bipedal, running and walking on two legs. Many of the bipedal dinosaurs were carnivores. By evolving as bipedal hunters, meat-eaters were not only fast but had front arms free for grabbing prey.

Perhaps the fastest of all were a family of dinosaurs called ornithomimids (or-nith-o-MIME-ids) or "bird mimics." *Struthiomimus* (strooth-ee-o-MIME-us) belonged to this family. They looked a lot like ostriches with powerful back legs and long slender necks held high. They might have eaten seeds and fruit and used their speed to hunt insects, small reptiles, and mammals.

We can estimate from the shape of dinosaur skeletons and the distance between fossilized footprints how fast dinosaurs ran. Paleontologists can also enter this information into computer programs to create simulations of how dinosaurs moved.

Struthiomimus may have run as fast as ostriches and racehorses, up to 45 mph! But even these hunters could become a tasty meal to larger carnivores. They needed to run fast to survive!

R r

R is for Run

You stalk your prey on two swift legs,
hoping that the chase won't last.
But now beware! Forget your prey!
Run! Run very FAST!

S is for Sky

Hunting, fishing, soaring, flapping
with giant wings and jaws snapping!
Deadly dragons really did fly,
as Pterosaurs in an ancient sky.

The Mesozoic sky was probably much the same as it is today, with sunny skies in good weather, and storm clouds, lightning, and high winds when it rained. However, that sky was ruled by pterosaurs (TERR-o-SORES).

Pterosaurs probably hunted fish, insects, small reptiles, mammals, and perhaps even ate seeds and berries. They could be as small as sparrows on up to the size of glider planes. There were two major groups: Rhamphorhynchoidea and Pterodactyloidea.

Rhamphorhynchoidea (RAM-for-ink-OID-ee-uh) had long tails, short necks, and sharp teeth to snag prey as they flew. They were the first pterosaurs to take to the sky. Pterodactyloidea (terro-DACK-till-OID-uh) evolved later and had short tails, longer necks, and were generally larger, such as *Criorhynchus* (cry-or-INK-us). Others had bony crests on their skulls and no teeth. The largest of all, *Quetzalcoatlus* (KWET-zal-KOH-at-luss), must have looked like a dragon in the air with its 40-foot wingspan.

Pterosaurs glided and flapped on wings made of tough, balloon rubber-like skin that stretched from their arms and extraordinarily long fourth finger to the side of the body and legs. Instead of scaly skin like reptiles, fossil imprints show their bodies were covered in fur, indicating they were warm-blooded.

Survival was difficult in the Mesozoic era. Dinosaurs evolved all sorts of adaptations to survive.

Dinosaurs that were too slow and heavy to outrun an attacker had no choice but to stay and defend themselves. Some, like *Ankylosaurus* (an-KIE-low-sore-us), were like walking fortresses, fully shielded by bony studs and armored plates. But their soft undersides were still open to attack, so they defended themselves with a clubbed tail of solid bone. This tail was as effective as a medieval mace. An attacking *Tyrannosaurus rex* was much taller, but had leg bones slender enough that it could have a leg broken by a powerful blow from that club tail. A broken leg could mean death even for the fiercest hunters.

Stegosaurus (steg-o-SORE-us) was another herbivore with a weapon for a tail. They had heavy bodies and were not built for speed. Their only defense against attack from ferocious *Allosaurus* (allo-SORE-us) was a tail armed with four sharp spikes. They swung their tails back and forth, aiming for the slender legs and soft underbelly of their attacker.

T is for Tails

Powerful tails,
bone-crushing tails—
Foot-breaking, leg-smashing,
spike-wielding TAILS!

U is for the Unknown

Many facts about dinosaurs may never be known.
How much can you know from studying a bone?
What color was their skin? Were they friendly or mean?
Were they covered in mud or spotlessly clean?

A fossil hunter once made an honest mistake when he thought he had discovered the largest dinosaur ever, *Ultrasaurus* (ultra-SORE-us). But the bones he found turned out to be bones from two dinosaurs already discovered, *Brachiosaurus* (brack-ee-o-SORE-us) and *Supersaurus* (SOO-per-SORE-us). Mistakes like this are easy to make because complete skeletons are rarely found. Paleontologists must piece together clues. Much about dinosaurs still remains unknown.

We may never know what color dinosaurs were, but by looking at animals alive today, we can make good guesses. Perhaps some dinosaurs were camouflaged in colors and patterns to help them blend into their surroundings. Others may have been brightly colored for attracting a mate.

When *Stegosaurus* (steg-o-SORE-us) was discovered, scientists first thought the bony plates laid flat along its back. Now we are fairly certain they sat upright, but we still don't understand their purpose. Birds today use color to identify their own species and win mates. Perhaps the plates were brightly colored so one *Stegosaurus* could recognize another.

U u

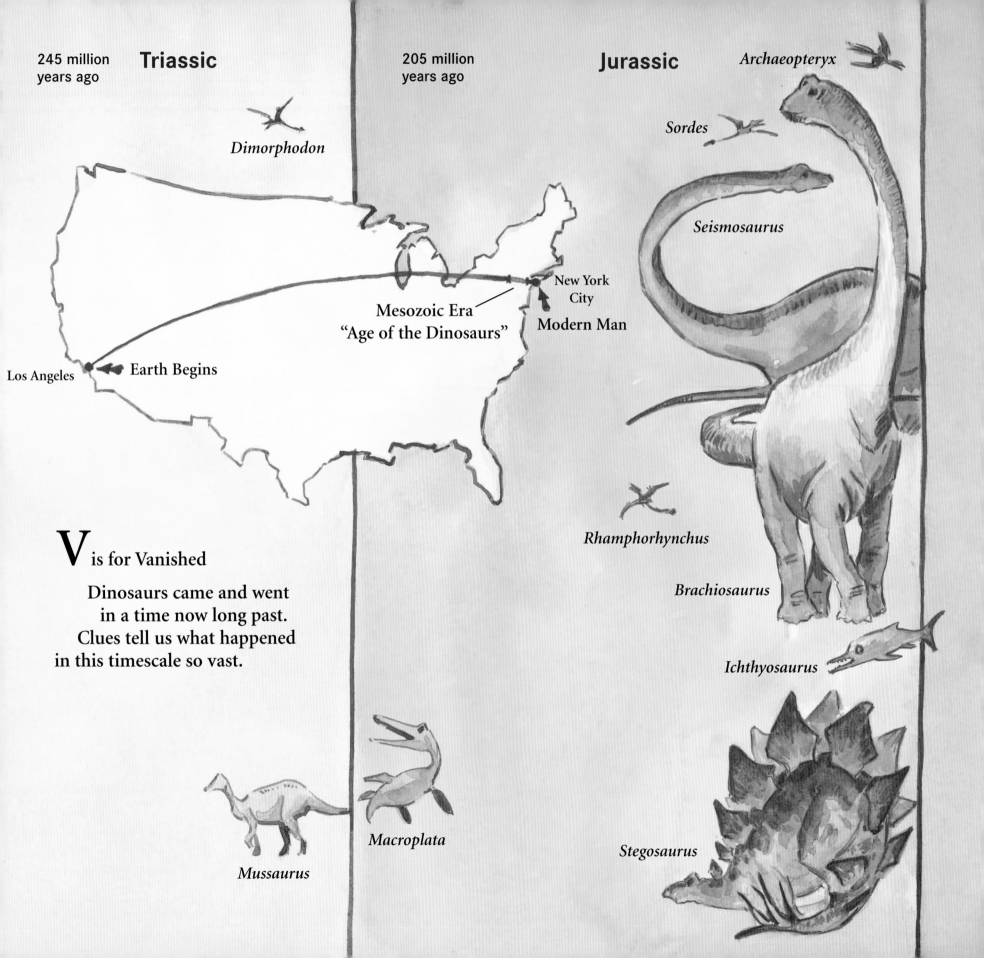

245 million years ago

Triassic

205 million years ago

Jurassic

Dimorphodon

Archaeopteryx

Sordes

Seismosaurus

Mesozoic Era "Age of the Dinosaurs"

New York City

Modern Man

Los Angeles   Earth Begins

Rhamphorhynchus

Brachiosaurus

Ichthyosaurus

V is for Vanished

Dinosaurs came and went
in a time now long past.
Clues tell us what happened
in this timescale so vast.

Macroplata

Mussaurus

Stegosaurus

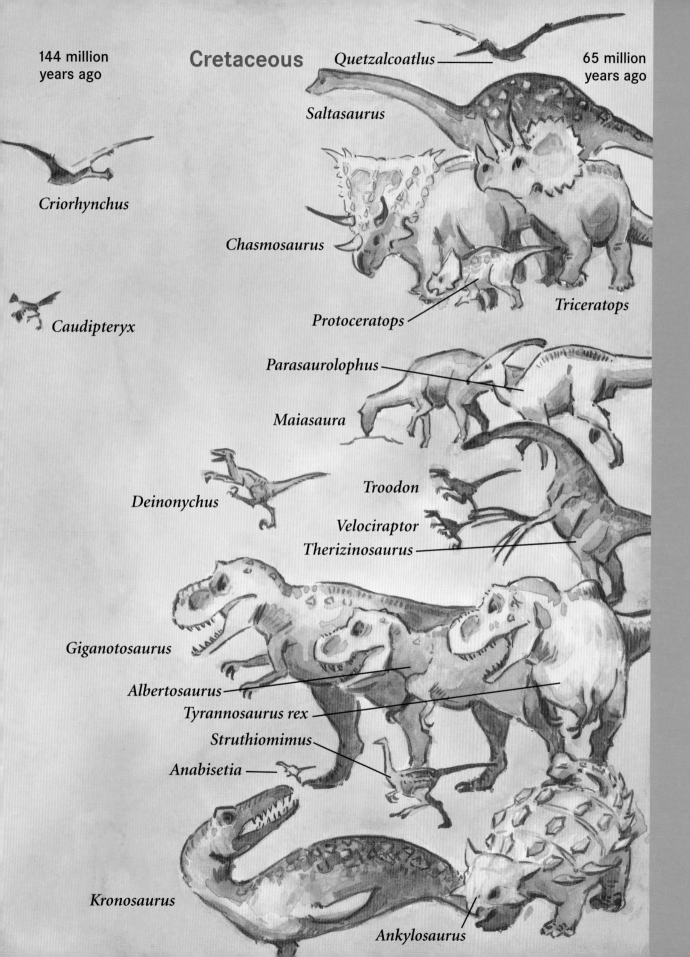

144 million years ago

65 million years ago

Cretaceous

Quetzalcoatlus

Saltasaurus

Criorhynchus

Chasmosaurus

Caudipteryx

Triceratops

Protoceratops

Parasaurolophus

Maiasaura

Troodon

Deinonychus

Velociraptor

Therizinosaurus

Giganotosaurus

Albertosaurus

Tyrannosaurus rex

Struthiomimus

Anabisetia

Kronosaurus

Ankylosaurus

We understand time passing in days, months, and years. The length of time that has passed since Earth was formed can be difficult to imagine; billions of years. Geologists understand time by dividing it into intervals determined by changes in fossils and rock layers in the earth's crust. These clues measure geological time.

In 1913 Arthur Holmes, a British geologist, introduced the first geologic timescale. It divides the earth's past into large intervals called eons that have, in turn, been divided into eras, eras into periods, and periods into epochs. By measuring the radioactive decay of certain elements within rocks (radioisotope dating), Holmes estimated that our planet was four billion years old. The geologic timescale has been modified as more knowledge was gained. Scientists now think the earth is just over 4.5 billion years old, but Holmes's scale remains a clear way to define geologic time.

Imagine the distance from Los Angeles to New York City as a geologic timescale. Dinosaurs evolved around Harrisburg, Pennsylvania. Modern man appeared about 50,000 years ago, or at the George Washington Bridge.

W is for Waterhouse Hawkins

The crowd gasped with awed delight
to witness such an incredible sight.
Waterhouse Hawkins hosted a feast
inside his model of a prehistoric beast.

In the mid-1800s most people had no idea what dinosaurs looked like. But a British sculptor named Benjamin Waterhouse Hawkins decided to show them. He built life-sized models of dinosaurs out of cement and steel. Hawkins had studied art, but also natural history and geology, giving him unique skills to model prehistoric animals. He also worked closely with the anatomist Richard Owen, the man who first coined the word dinosaur.

The models took three years to build. On New Year's Eve in 1853 Hawkins hosted an elegant dinner party inside a life-sized *Iguanodon* (ig-WAHN-o-don), inviting 21 of the world's prominent scientists. Eventually the dinosaur models were put on display in the Sydenham Park of the Crystal Palace in London. Forty thousand spectators came, even the Queen of England, for the unveiling. The models were so popular, many credit Hawkins with starting the fascination we all have with dinosaurs.

Hawkins was an artist, but he worked closely with scientists of his time. This tradition continues today in paleontology. The next time you visit a museum or read a book, remember that scientists rely on artists to bring prehistoric creatures to life.

W
W
W

Nearing the end of the Cretaceous period, more dinosaurs than ever walked the land. But by the very end of the period, 65 million years ago, no dinosaurs (except the birds) existed. Pterosaurs and large marine reptiles were also gone. What could have caused such a mass planet extinction? Scientists have argued about this for decades.

Some scientists think the extinction happened gradually over time from disease, climate changes, and atmospheric poisoning by volcanic eruptions. But there is growing evidence that a meteorite or similar object hit Earth, creating a sudden, catastrophic change to its climate.

The impact of such a massive meteorite would have instantly wiped out life within hundreds of miles from the crash site. Intense heat from the strike would have started fires burning out of control. Huge amounts of ash and debris would have been thrown into the atmosphere, blocking out sunlight for months. Debris from the impact would have caused acid rain, perhaps poisoning the air. Little sunlight and a cold climate would cause plant life to die, leaving little food for the herbivores. As the herbivores died, the carnivores, with no food source, also died.

X
X

X is for eXtinction

One big question still remains:
Where did the dinosaurs go?
There are many theories
but we don't exactly know.

Y y

Y is for the Yucatan

Did a comet hit the Earth?
One big crater gives a clue.
Could the end have come so fast?
Many scientists think it's true.

The meteorite theory had much evidence to support it when physicist Luis Alvarez and his son Walter, a geologist, proposed it in 1980. But no impact site for such a huge meteorite was known, so scientists began looking for one.

In 1990 Alan Hildebrand discovered evidence of an enormous impact crater while examining scientific data originally collected for finding oil. The crater is at least one mile deep and 112 miles wide! It lies at the northwest tip of the Yucatan Peninsula within the Gulf of Mexico. With further study of the area, scientists found both chemical and physical evidence to suggest that this was the spot. It was formed about 65 million years ago, just about when the mass extinction occurred.

The village of Chicxulub (CHIK-shoo-loob) is thought to be the actual site where the big one hit!!! Can you guess the name of the impact crater?

Zuniceratops (ZOO-nee-SERRA-tops) was a ceratopsian dinosaur, like *Triceratops* (try-SERRA-tops). It had a skull with a large bony frill over its neck. But *Zuniceratops* was only about ten feet long, three feet high, and weighed 200 pounds. The first skeleton was found by eight-year-old Christopher James Wolfe in New Mexico.

Paleontologists go prospecting for fossils by walking through landscapes where they know the ground is rich in fossils. The best time to look is after rain has washed away dirt and possibly exposed another great fossil. There are places you can visit to see dinosaur fossils. Two of the greatest fossil sites in the world are Dinosaur National Monument in Utah and Dinosaur Provincial Park in Alberta, Canada. Here you can see dinosaur fossils in place and watch paleontologists and assistants work to excavate them.

Dinosaur National Monument includes a fossil quarry and visitor center near Jensen, Utah. Here you can see over 1,400 exposed dinosaur fossils. The bonebed, with its amazing concentration of dinosaurs, was discovered by Earl Douglas in 1909. In 1915 President Woodrow Wilson proclaimed the dinosaur-rich beds a National Monument. The monument was expanded to its current size of 200,000 acres in 1938 to include land on the border of Utah and Colorado.

Zz

Z is for Zuniceratops

Not long ago
our letter Z was discovered,
when an eight-year-old boy
found *Zuniceratops* uncovered.

Early in the 1900s "The Great Canadian Dinosaur Rush" brought paleontologists to the Red Deer Valley in Alberta, Canada. Scientists like Barnum Brown and Charles Sternberg searched for dinosaurs in the fossil-rich badlands. In 1955 Dinosaur Provincial Park was established. Fossilized fish, sharks, amphibians, turtles, crocodiles, lizards, and about 40 different dinosaur species have been found there. The park is recognized by the United Nations as a World Heritage Site and is a protected research area.

In 1985 the Royal Tyrell Museum of Paleontology opened in nearby Drumheller. It's named in honor of Joseph Tyrell, the geologist who originally discovered the first *Albertosaurus* (al-bert-o-SORE-us) in this valley. Today the museum has more than 200 dinosaur specimens on display and can be visited year-round.

Artwork Explanations From A to Z

A—Anning: Mary Anning excavates an ichthyosaur skeleton

B—Bonebed: A *Chasmosaurus* bonebed gives clues that a herd drowned in a flood

C—Claws: *Therizinosaurus* chases a family of *Oviraptors*

D—Dinosaurs: Saurischian (lizard hipped) and Ornithischian (bird hipped) dinosaur chart

E—Evolution: *Troodon* dinosaurs hunt small mammals

F—Feathers: *Caudipteryx,* a feathered dinosaur

G—Gigantic: Two *Giganotosaurus* chase two small *Anabisetia* dinosaurs

H—Herds of Herbivores: A *Sordes* flies over a herd of sauropod dinosaurs

I—Intruder: Two *Parasaurolophus* are alerted to a stalking dromaeosorid

J—Jurassic Giraffes: *Brachiosaurus* eat from the treetops

K—King: Family of *Tyrannosaurus rex* chase a *Quetzalcoatlus*

L & M—Littlest & Good Mother Lizard: *Maiasaura* mother and babies

N—Nest: *Saltasaurus* babies with adults in the background

O—Oceans: A *Kronosaurus* in the foreground, two plesiosaurs in the background

P—Paleontologist: Paleontologists assemble a *Tyrannosaurus rex* skeleton

Q—Quadruped: *Protoceratops* grips the arm of *Velociraptor*

R—Run: *Albertosaurus* chases two *Struthiomimus*

S—Sky: *Criorhynchus*

T—Tails: *Ankylosaurus* battles *Tyrannosaurus rex*

U—Unknown: Two *Stegosaurus*

V—Vanished: Chart showing when the dinosaurs depicted in this book lived

W—Waterhouse Hawkins: The New Year's Eve party Waterhouse Hawkins held in his model of *Iguanodon*

X & Y—Extinct & Yucatan: A *Triceratops* skeleton

Z—Zuniceratops: Christopher James Wolfe uncovers the skeleton of *Zuniceratops*